Merry Christmas

I Spy Christmas Book for Kids: Stocking Stuffers for Kids

LITTLE NOEL PRESS

I Spy with my little eye something beginning with...

Angel

I Spy with my little eye something beginning with...

Bag

I Spy with my little eye something beginning with...

Cranberries

I Spy with my little eye something beginning with...

Dog

I Spy with my little eye something beginning with...

Elf

I Spy with my little eye something beginning with...

Fireplace

I Spy with my little eye something beginning with...

Gingerbread house

I Spy with my little eye something beginning with...

Hot chocolate

I Spy with my little eye something beginning with...

Ice skates

I Spy with my little eye something beginning with...

Jingle bells

I Spy with my little eye something beginning with...

Kite

I Spy with my little eye something beginning with...

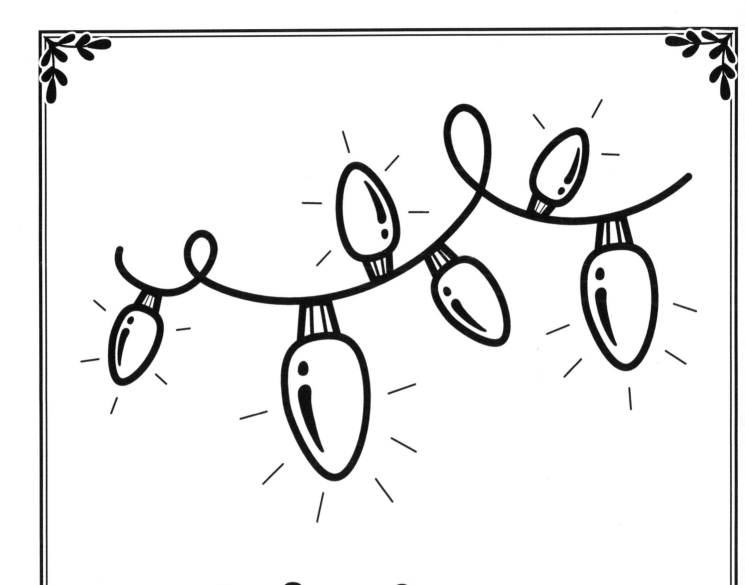

Lights

I Spy with my little eye something beginning with...

Mittens

I Spy with my little eye something beginning with...

Nutcracker

I Spy with my little eye something beginning with...

Ornaments

I Spy with my little eye something beginning with...

Plum Pudding

I Spy with my little eye something beginning with...

۲

Queen

I Spy with my little eye something beginning with...

Reindeer

I Spy with my little eye something beginning with...

Santa Claus

I Spy with my little eye something beginning with...

Teddy bear

٢

I Spy with my little eye something beginning with...

Unicorn

I Spy with my little eye something beginning with...

Van

I Spy with my little eye something beginning with...

Wreath

I Spy with my little eye something beginning with...

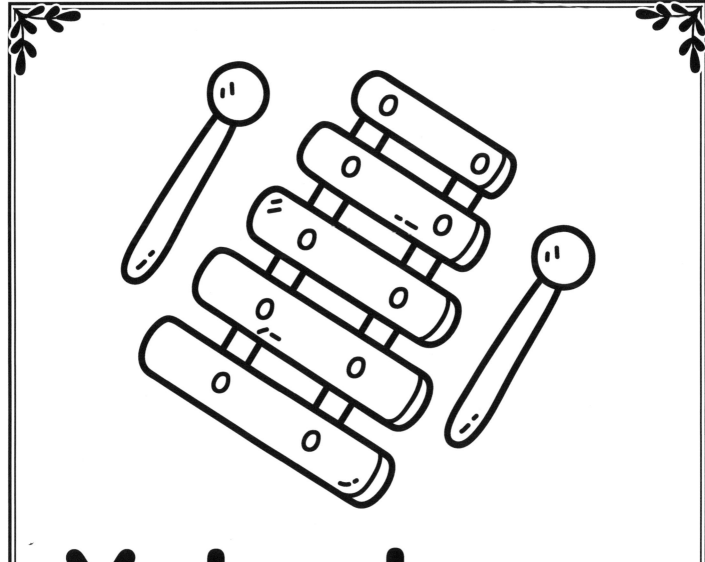

Xylophone

I Spy with my little eye something beginning with...

Yoyo

I Spy with my little eye something beginning with...

Zebra

Made in the USA
Monee, IL
25 November 2024

71155970R00059